Kuzen Azaka Mede
Engaging with the Lwa of
Work, Labor, and Land

I0101420

Kuzen Azaka Mede: Engaging with the Lwa of Work, Labor, and Land

Copyright © 2022 Joseph Alexander Robicheaux
Cover Image © Marcos Rivard
Published by Hadean Press
West Yorkshire
www.hadeanpress.com

ISBN 978-1-914166-01-3

Kuzen Azaka Mede
Engaging with the Lwa of Work, Labor, and Land

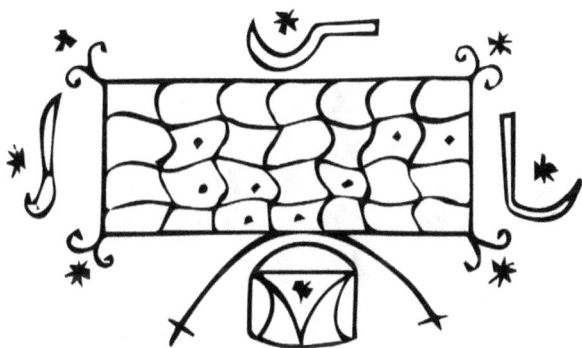

Ya Sezi bo Oungan
(Joseph Alexander Robicheaux)

Thank you

Kuzen Azaka Mede
Marie Andre Kasekan Bo Mambo
Adé oké Jesse Obatala
Osunletilewa Jose Ochun
Lucian Van Vanté Bo Oungan
Steven Twa po Terre Bo Oungan
Toby Chá Ché Maché Bo Oungan
Jesse Yasezi Bo Oungan
Draoi Lora O'Brien
All my God Kids...
Jesse Alotto and Shane Lemoine

This book is dedicated to:
The Tuscarora Nation, and the Haudenosaunee Five
Nations People, who were the first to instruct me in the
terrors and ways of the colonizers and invaders.
To the souls of the Tainos, Arawaks, Caribs, Ciboney, and
all the native people of North, South, Central America,
and the Caribbean killed, injured, disconnected, kidnapped
by colonizers, from first contact to this very day.
To all the missing and murdered Indigenous women of
Canada, you are not forgotten. And in recognition of
the continued aggravated aggression and racism of the
Canadian Government against its First Nations people.
To all the lost, and Federally unrecognized tribes like the
Lumbee People of North Carolina, Biloxi People, Hasinai
people, Yazoo People, Tunica People, and the
Houma Nation of the Gulf Coast.
And to Boriken, the island of Puerto Rico will be free of
all Colonial powers and shall be self-governing again.

Contents

Taino by C. Huerra

Introduction by Oungan Hector

Alaso, Alaso Kouzen and
Alaso YaSezi Bon Oungan

This book contains a wealth of information about one of the most important and foundational spirits in Haitian Vodou, Kouzen Zaka. Kouzen is a powerful and loyal ally who can greatly improve your life if he chooses to work with you. However, even if he doesn't, his wisdom can help you transform many aspects of your life.

Kouzen is the spirit of work and agriculture. His wisdom gives insight into this arena of life and how to make it work. Solidly connected with the Earth, which we all call home, Kouzen shows the path to live in harmony. A hardworking farmer, he teaches how to plant and manifest a life of simplicity, care and devotion.

In Haiti, Kouzen is a very well known, regularly served, and important Lwa. Many people are devoted and connected to him. In the diaspora, however, there is a gap and disconnect with him due to environmental and cultural differences. However, in this book, Ya Sezi helps to fill in that gap. By doing so, he gives those in the diaspora a better view of Kouzen but also of his fundamental role in Vodou and Vodou culture.

Closely related and connected to the Djouba are the practices and cultures of the Tainos. In fact, you can't fully discuss Kouzen without mentioning them. Here Ya Sezi will help you connect the dots as well as give you a foundation and introduction to the Tainos.

Within these pages, novices and practitioners alike will find great information on the Djouba nation of Vodou. With discussion as to its specific terminology as well as various mysteries within the nation, a thorough groundwork is provided. So many aspects of this rarely discussed group are covered.

Along with historical and insightful facts about Kouzen and the Djouba, offerings, workings, tools, and more are given to get you started, should this Lwa be with you. Ya Sezi has given a great introduction, primer, and resource for those who are interested in Vodou or Kouzen.

Oungan Hector

In the Beginning

Before France, before the horrors of Triangle Trade, or Columbus and the Caribbean native Tainos, there was Atabey, the cosmic water and frog mother, who created the heavens. However, there was still an emptiness; something was still missing within the nothingness, where nothingness prevailed. In this nothingness all things were fixed in inaction. The heavens were inactive, and any action was meaningless. Earth and the other cosmic entities lay barren. Despite being dominated by darkness, Atabey herself failed to notice that this universe was incomplete and did not see a problem with the inaction of the cosmos. Eventually she decided to create two new deities, Yucáhu and Guacar, from light, sound, matter, magic, and from intangible elements. Atabey now felt sure that her creation could be completed and left it in the charge of her two sons. Yucáhu took over as a deity of creation, becoming a universal architect and gathering the favor of his mother.

From his dwelling in the heavens, he contemplated and awoke the Earth from its slumber, and as part of this process, two new deities emerged from a cave. Boinael and Maroya, controlling the sun and moon respectively, were tasked with illuminating day and night in this new world. No longer would the Earth be shrouded by darkness. Yucáhu was satisfied with his work, but, in a fit of jealousy, Guacar hid within the heavens, never to be seen again. Now bored, Yucáhu roamed and noticed four gemstones that resided in the now awakened Earth, which he took and converted into the celestial star beings Racuno, Sobaco, Achinao and Coromo, who reproduced and spread throughout the universe, where they guide the zemi.

He followed this by creating animals, granting them dwellings and teaching them how to live. Yucáhu then had a revelation, believing that something else should complete his creation. Convinced that the new entity should be neither animal nor deity, he pondered this profoundly. Yucáhu then opened a rift in the heavens from which emerged the first man, whom he granted a soul and named Locuo. This man would roam the Earth endlessly, filled with joy and thanking the deity for his creation. Finally, satisfied with his creation, Yucáhu left the world to rest in his home on top of El Younque. Trusting in Locuo and with the Earth in the hands of humanity, he felt that a balance had been reached. Was balance reached?

The voices of the colonized are dampened by the roaring of the machines and machinations of the treacherous, and the same is true of their histories, accomplishments, and their entire cultures' future impact on their world. It is far too polite to say history is told by the victors, when they cheated and lied while being led by endless avarice, religious bloodlust, and near endless racist rapine upon the other people of the world.

'In 1492 Columbus sailed the ocean blue', as the elementary school song goes. The Nina, the Pinta, and the first shipwreck in North America, the Santa Maria, were ships under the patronage of Queen Isabella of Spain. Just after reclaiming Granada from the Moors, Spain was primed for the next conquest, since its home territory had been reclaimed after a 780-year war. This war had been fought between Christians, Jews, and Muslims, and Europeans, Africans, and Asians, over the ownership of and right to exist in the Iberian Peninsula. In 1492 the last and only Moorish fortress in Spain, the Alhambra in Granada, remained. By this time, political pressure and dynastic marriages had unified Spain and turned it into a formidable European power. With the last step in the taking of Spain complete, the prospect of a 'New World' seemed a ripe opportunity, and Spain, favorite of the Vatican, had the financial ability to fund what was originally a trade expedition, and which would become the great search for passage to the East, ultimately hoping to find India by travelling westwards, and to arrive in the East by means of our oblate spheroid planet.

> YOUR HIGHNESSES, as Catholic Christians and Princes who love the holy Christian faith, and the propagation of it, and who are enemies to the sect of Mahoma [Islam] and to all idolatries and heresies, resolved to send me, Cristóbal Colon, to the said parts of India to see the said princes […] with a view that they might be converted to our holy faith […] Thus, after having turned out all the Jews from all your kingdoms and lordships […] your Highnesses gave orders to me that with a sufficient fleet I

should go to the said parts of India [...]
I shall forget sleep, and shall work at the
business of navigation, so that the service is performed.

– Christopher Columbus[1]

Many attempts were made by so-called
explorers to find a shorter and more direct route
to India and the Far East. Christopher Columbus
attempted to go west in order to go east. Many
people held strange notions as to what was going
on far beyond their charted waters. Dragons,
demons, Hy Brazil, and many other beings and
mysterious places were considered more than
likely possible discoveries. Instead there were
no dragons, no demons, no Hy Brazil; there
were only the unforgiving and rugged lands that
would be known in the future as the Greater
and Lesser Antilles, and these lands' people, the
Native Americans of the Caribbean.

Dubbed *Hispaniola*, or 'Little Spain', by
Columbus, it was then known to the residents of
this island as *Ayiti*, 'the land of tall mountains' or

---

1 *The Northmen, Columbus, and Cabot, 985-1503: The
Voyages of the Northmen, the Voyages of Columbus and of
John Cabot*, ed. by E. G. Bourne and J. E. Olson (New
York: Charles Scribner's Sons, 1906), pp. 90-91.

Quisqueya, 'Mother of all Islands', in the language of native people of the Greater Antilles, commonly called the Taino and Arawaks. This island was split into five kingdoms or *Casica* or *cacicazgos*, known by the Latinized names Jaragua in the southwest, Maguana in the central south, Higüey in the furthest west, Maguá in the north-west, and Marièn in the north-east. Each was led by a chieftain or *cacique*. The island had a unique form of governance that did not allow for one biological gender to have total political control.

During the time of the Spanish invasion, the caciques were made up of one woman to four men. The five caciques at the time of the invasion of the Spanish were Guacanagrix of Marièn, Anacaona of Jaragua, Canabo of Maguana, Cotubanama of Higüey, and Guarionex of Maguá. Christopher Columbus wrecked his ship in the kingdom of Marièn, where the natives assisted him and his people. From his wrecked ship Columbus and his crew built the first European structure on the island. On Christmas day this fort was complete, a large Christmas feast was prepared, and a meal was shared between the Spanish and the natives, beginning the tale of tragic misery and woe known as Colonialism in this region. The fort

Kuzen Azaka Mede

was La Navidad, at Puerto la Navidad, in what is now the City of Cap-Haitien. The primary interest of the Spanish, other than conversion of the indigenous peoples to Christianity, was the search for gold.

> They... brought us parrots and balls of cotton and spears and many other things, which they exchanged for the glass beads and hawks' bells. They willingly traded everything they owned... They were well-built, with good bodies and handsome features... They do not bear arms, and do not know them, for I showed them a sword, they took it by the edge and cut themselves out of ignorance. They have no iron. Their spears are made of cane... They would make fine servants... With fifty men we could subjugate them all and make them do whatever we want.
>
> – Christopher Columbus[2]

---

2 Howard Zinn, *A People's History of the United States* (Harlow: Longman Group, 1980), p. 1.

Christopher Columbus left thirty Spanish people to man La Navidad who began acting out, raping, enslaving, and subjugating the Taino Arawak people, forcing them into mining and farming, and taking advantage of their peacefulness. The Carib nation, who before the arrival of the Spanish existed in the Lesser Antilles and in coastal areas around modern-day Trinidad and Tobago, later joined forces with the Taino people against their common enemy. The Carib people, in comparison to the Taino, were much more war-like.

The caciques of Ayiti – Anacaona, Canabo, and Guacangrix – formed a raiding party and razed fort La Navidad to the ground, killing all of its European occupants. On 27 November 1493, Christopher Columbus returned to his colony to find only ruins. This time he did not have such a small group of men with him, but had brought with him conquistadors of much repute who were bloodthirsty for war and combat now that Spain had been 'reclaimed' from the presence of Muslims and Jews. They brought with them women, many priests and religious professionals, and trade specialists. He also brought the first European large-breed dogs, including mastiffs and the excessively cute and vilified pit bull, as well as horses, cows, pigs, chickens, and a slew of other non-native lifeforms including illnesses, while above all their steel weapons and gunpowder were their most deadly weapons. Since the fort La Navidad was no more, he established a new fort not far from Puerto La Navidad at a place called La Isabel in the modern-day Dominican Republic.

From this point forward, the Spanish interactions with the indigenous population were, to say the least, cruel and terrible. Wholesale massacre and genocide were committed against them. Quotas were imposed on them; punishment for not filling a quota was mutilation and dismemberment. A system known as *Encomienda* was imposed upon them. This system worked by requiring the indigenous people to pay a fee for protection by a Spanish Encomendero, like a mob-style shake down. This was done in many places, but ultimately it was established and made common practice in Hispaniola by the new governor, Nicolás de Ovando, after Christopher Columbus had been arrested by Franciso de Bobadilla for gross incompetence in the management of the island.

Ovando was not known for his generosity and humanity. In 1502, when Nicolás de Ovando arrived in Hispaniola, the once peaceful island and its inhabitants were in revolt. Spain had seen enough of the Columbus governorship to know that he was not productive or helpful to the process, and so had him replaced with a man who was possibly even more evil. The caciques, being honorable, petitioned the new governor to speak to the king. In particular, Canabo and his brother Manicatex asked to speak to the king of the Spanish, to inform him of the misrule and mismanagement of the island, the brutal subjugation of the people, and the total disrespect shown to their way of life.

They were greeted with manacles and chains, said to be gifts from the king, which led to their capture. The Spanish plan was to send Canabo and his brother to Spain. There are many tales of these two brave and honorable people which all end the same: they never make it alive to Europe. The most endearing version is that they broke free of their chains and the ship was lost in a storm, never to be seen again.

> While I was in the boat, I captured a very beautiful Carib woman, whom the said Lord Admiral [Christopher Columbus] gave to me. When I had taken her to

my cabin she was naked—as was their custom. I was filled with a desire to take my pleasure with her and attempted to satisfy my desire. She was unwilling, and so treated me with her nails that I wished I had never begun. But—to cut a long story short—I then took a piece of rope and whipped her soundly, and she let forth such incredible screams that you would not have believed your ears. Eventually we came to such terms, I assure you, that you would have thought that she had been brought up in a school for whores.

- Michele de Cuneo, friend and travelling companion of Columbus[3]

<hr />

3 Michele de Cuneo, (1495) *Letter to Lord Hieronymo Annari*, 28 October.

Anakaona the Golden Flower, Cacique of Jaragua

When they saw who was sitting on the throne it was as bright as the sun, and people raised their hands in praise, "who is that?" they asked [...] "Anacaona [...] our Queen.
– Bartolomé de las Casas, *The History of the Indies*

Amongst all the caciques of Hispaniola, none was more of a thorn in the side of the Spanish than the last Queen of the Taino in Jaragua, Anacaona, the Golden Flower, who ruled from what is today Léogâne, Haiti. Anacaona was from a royal lineage of female rulership, and her brother and husband were among the chief caciques of the island. It was customary that there should be at least one cacique of the opposite biological gender for balance, so at no point could there be all male caciques, neither could they be all female.

Detail from 'Honors to Queen Anacaona', from *Vida y viajes de Cristóbal Colón*, Madrid: Impr. de Gaspar y Roig, 1852

According to some historians, the natives of the Greater Antilles traced lineage matrilineally. Anacaona's grandmother, mother, and brother were all caciques before her. During her time on the Island of Boriken, or Puerto Rico, there was another female cacique named Luisa, or Yuisa. Anacaona was renowned throughout the modern Caribbean. She was a poet and was famous for her religious ballads and narrative poems and sacred dances, dedicated to the ancestors and zemi called *Areitos*. She was a *bohique*, a religious expert and a priestess, and a shaman. Her athleticism and skill as a warrior were also of renown. Anacaona married another cacique who was of similar standing to her, named Conabo. Anacaona welcomed all renegades, defectors, and runaways to her cause, and would launch guerrilla style attacks against the Spanish.

After the stolen sovereignty of the island was taken from Christopher Columbus by his Spanish financiers and handed over to Nicolás de Ovando, Anacaona and her brother, the former Cacique for Jaragua, made moves to welcome the new governor and to have peace talks. A banquet was prepared, and dancers and poets were present to regale their foreign overlords at the *batey* or longhouse. The peace talks were

Kuzen Azaka Mede

documented by a figure we have yet to discuss, Bartolomé de Las Casas, a Dominican Friar and the first to be ordained a Catholic priest in the Americas. This peace talk was held in the longhouse of Anacaona, and eighty of the Taino chiefs were present that day.

> With my own eyes I saw Spaniards cut off the nose and ears of Indians, male and female, without provocation, merely because it pleased them to do it. Likewise, I saw how they summoned the caciques and the chief rulers to come, assuring them safety, and when they peacefully came, they were taken captive and burned.
> – Bartolomé de las Casas, *A Short Account of the Destruction of the Indies*

The only honest people at this meeting were the Taino, who only wanted to discuss, and come to terms for, lasting peace, while also not accepting total domination by the Spanish. Ovando and the Spanish had an alternative plan: they prepared a sign whereby Ovando would touch his crucifix, which would indicate that the Spanish were to leave the longhouse with Anacaona as their prisoner. They were to then bar the doors and set her longhouse on fire. Anyone who attempted to escape the blaze was shot. The charge was for crimes of witchcraft, attempting to seduce both Spanish and natives to join her cause when she led the rebellion, and of sedition and rebellion against Spanish rule. They offered her clemency if she would abdicate her power and become a concubine to one of the Spanish officers. To these crimes and to the offensive terms of clemency Anacaona conceded, accepting her fate, allegedly answering with the following verse: 'It is not honorable to kill; nor can honor propitiate tragedy. Let us open a bridge of love, so that across it even our enemies may walk and leave for posterity their footprints'. In 1503 Anacaona was hanged by the neck until dead. She was twenty-nine years old.

☙

Bartolomé de Las Casas was the first Catholic to be ordained a priest in North America. He was a Dominican friar, author and transcriber, known for his copy of Columbus's diary, and one of the few Europeans to fight for fair treatment of the Natives. He wrote many books, amongst them *A Short Account of the Destruction of the Indies* and *The History of the Indies*, in which he details the disposition of the native peoples and the treatment of the natives by the Spanish. He also critiqued Christianity's, and Christian's morality.

> Their reason for killing and destroying such an infinite number of souls is that the Christians have an ultimate aim, which is to acquire gold, and to swell themselves with riches in a very brief time and thus rise to a high estate disproportionate to their merits... It should be kept in mind that their insatiable greed and ambition, the greatest ever seen in the world, is the cause of their villainies.
> – Bartolomé de las Casas, *The History of the Indies*

Bartolomé was not a totally innocent person, for in his defense of the native people he made a perhaps accidental and foolish suggestion that would ultimately be followed, and from that choice to this time, would cause these keystrokes of mine to be made. Bartolomé suggested that to save the native population, Africans should be enslaved and brought to Hispaniola to toil. It is true that West Africans did have a higher survival rate, mostly due to having already been exposed to Old World diseases like smallpox, to which the native people did not have any form of immunity. It is known that he greatly regretted his words on the enslavement of the Africans. In 1515 Bartolomé had an audience with King Ferdinand of Spain, arguing the issues of slavery and the freedoms of the native people. Ultimately Bartolomé de las Casas began the now 500-year-old journey of human rights, after spurring it into existence. Bartolomé's talks with King Ferdinand spurred other theologians, and many scientists, to discuss the humanity of the native people of the 'new world'.

Another important person, who was also a first, was Ramón Pané, who recorded much of what we know about the culture and customs of the Taino people, including their religious and spiritual articles, often referred to as *cemi* or *zemi*. *Zemi* are linked to ancestors, and all have various powers and attributes. Some were worn and carried, while others were enshrined in *calabashes* and secured within private homes. One of the most common *zemi* found is the triangular, three-cornered stone, called *trogonalitos* by the Spanish.

Carved on one side with a face, these were buried in the ground where yucca was growing to help ensure healthy growth. Once a year clothing would be made for the *zemi*, and cassava bread would be baked and offered to the ancestors and the *zemi*, while *areíto* were being performed for them.

When looking at the surface of the spiritual practice and interactions of the Taino's spirituality through the eyes of the Spanish, there are many similarities that can be drawn between the native people and the Africans. There are four features that are shared: things we can ascertain from what oral tradition, written record, and living traditions survive of the extant Taino people.

- Religious worship and obeisance to the *zemi* themselves
- The performance of *areítos*, recitation of poetry, song, and dancing in the village court during special festivals of thanksgiving or petition
- Medicine men, or priests, consulting the *zemi* for advice and healing.
- Public ceremonies with song and dance, ritual sacrifice, and a communal meal.

Sounds like a Vodou Party if you ask me!

The *Bohiques* and *Nitaynos,* or medicine priests, wore ceremonial attire. Bedecked in shells from the knees down, they would paint their bodies with pigments and wear feathers, bones, and other distinguishing found items relating to their spiritual tradition. They would bring out the carved *zemi* and present them to the cacique, who would be seated on a stool in a place of honor. Poems and songs dedicated to the *zemi*, or to the *opia* or ancestors would be performed. The veneration of the ancestors is both a building block and foundation upon which they built their spirituality and life, as I talked about at length in my previous book, *Guede et Mo: A Workbook*. It is important to remember that the ancestors and the Lwa, while not (always) being the same, are connected.

Kuzen Azaka Mede

The Djouba or Djumba Nation

Taino, and African, from the Bight of Benin to Ayiti, traveling far to accomplish much, you are known for your peerless mastery of the earth, you are known as a provider and a hard worker. You are staunch and plain in matters of business, with an eye to know who can pay what and how, and most importantly when. You know the mysteries of how to make the earth reveal and provide its many treasures. Minister of the earth, you are the inheritor and instructor of the sacred dwelling of man.

The Djouba (pronounced ju-bah) people are from the region of Savalou Mayhi in Benin. Much like the Rada Nation, the Kongo, and the Ibo nations, the nation reflects the spirits that were from a specific place as well as referring to the ethnic group that venerated these spirits. The word Djouba also refers to the rhythms and dances used in the veneration of these spirits, like Djouba, Konbit, and Chawo pye.

The Djouba nation does not account for a great part of the Vodou ceremony but does hold a position of paramount importance. The Djouba are subsections of the Rada rite; unlike the Rada and the Petwo, they are not a gigantic variety of Lwa that accompany these mysteries. This is a smaller nation composed of more or less a single family of Lwa. These people had a very large swath of former and present-day Benin in the region known as Savalou Mayi of the Kingdom of Dahomey, areas near the *Kongo dia Ntotila* or the kingdom of the Kongo; later research links these people (and the Lwa) to Sierra Leone and the Ivory Coast. However, unlike other Lwa, the Djouba are not purely (or shall we say mostly) African. Native Americans of the Greater Antilles and South America, commonly referred to as Taino and Arawak people and culture, are also incorporated into these mysteries. How could they not be?

For a Lwa that has a relative relationship to this otherwise 'new' land (new to the African enslaved workers and the Europeans) it is only natural that the original inhabitants of *Hispaniola* could be found here. Some items that Kuzen is specifically known for have Taino origin, like his woven bag of palm fibers, called a *Makout* or

Kuzen Azaka Mede

Djakout; his love of tobacco; his palm fiber hat; and not to mention much of the food we refer to as 'Guinea food', a food from North America that was the primary staple of the enslaved people's diet.

Columbus and the Spaniards had a very poor idea of how to treat these individuals. Native Taino and Arawak people were treated with the same disrespect as the African peoples, and were sold into chattel slavery. The Taino and Arawak people knew the cultivars of the area; casaba, sugar and corn were among their usual crops. In much of Europe's interaction with the Native Americans, many miscommunications, deliberate or otherwise, took place. The way these people farmed did not make sense to the European mind that tore down the foraging forests and spread the style of growing a monoculture crop. The foods that were eaten by the enslaved people are known today as *Manje Guinea* or Guinea/African food. This list of foods is rather long. These items are commonly used in offerings made to many Lwa, not just Kuzen and the Djouba spirits.

Guinea foods as a list:

Peanuts
Spinach
Cassabas
Battata
Potatoes
Plantains
Okra
Honey
Mirlitons/Chayotes
Squash
Rice
Corn
Beans
Salt fish and meat
Bread
Sugar
Yams

Azaka Family Tree

Azaka Mede, Kuzen Azaka, and many of the Azaka family of spirits are politely known as Kouzen, which means cousin, and that is how I often refer to them in this book. It is good to know the members of the many greater families of Lwa in Vodou. It doesn't matter who has shown up – what matters is the respect that is due to the visiting Lwa. Only on the very personal level is it important (and sometimes it is not) to know the specifics. These Lwa reflect people's everyday culture in much of Haiti; moreover, the Djouba family of spirits give the ability for humanity to settle and establish themselves. They are the force that tames the wilderness and teaches the ways of plants and animals so that we can produce food, have large families, and prosper. Kuzen is a key part of the trinity of Lwa that are our journey in life.

Minis Tonner: The capacity for growth, the force for things to grow, the master of the skill to grow food on mountain sides. Is associated also with the thunder that precedes rain.

Azaka Si: The mystery of germination and plants, the gestation of a seed in the darkness of the soil taking root from a hard, dry, seemingly dead thing. They are the living seed that grows.

Azaka La: The green shoot that explodes from the ground, and from there grows. They are also the cultivar that grows in a strange place, especially where it is unexpected. Azaka Si and Azaka La in many ways are like the Marassa of the Azaka Lwa.

Minis Agwele: The Lwa of fresh water that brings life, the progenitive power of the rains, especially rain in May, and the Lwa of cultivar plants that grow in the water, like rice. The Lwa of the farmer-turned-merchant. He is a brother to Met Agwe.

Minis Dansi: A genderless water Lwa related to the Danbala Wedo.

Minis Azaka Tonner: Minis Azaka Tonner is the force that plows and turns and breaks the new soil — this force is incredibly old. He is the force that takes the wild and untamed land and makes it suitable to grow plants. He is the force that sets civilization moving, and that goes to battle with Gran Bwa, Lwa of the forest, over where the forest ends and the farmstead begins. This Lwa is the embodiment of the harsh challenges of farming in the mountains, hills, and stony places and making them functional spaces in which life can grow. Tonner is understood as thunder, this Lwa having a relationship with Sobo. This thundering would be the tearing up of roots and rocks, and the falling of trees. It is this Lwa who accepts the bodies of the deceased.

Azaka Krib: this Azaka is a hot Petwo Lwa. Instead of being bipedal and walking when mounted, they scoot around on their behinds with a *bouji*, a kind of candle that is made from twisted fabric, wax, lard, and other flammable materials, of which they can be seen rubbing the flaming portion on their feet. This is because this Azaka is afflicted with a foot illness caused by overexposure to moisture, something like an advanced case of trench foot.

Gran Adali Mede: Mother of Minis Azaka, wife of Papa Legba, she is the Lwa of boundaries and property stakes, which were especially important in the early development of the estate system used in Haiti and many locations in the new world. She is also the Lwa who is the cane or crutch of Papa Legba. If Legba is the threshold, Gran Adali Mede is the boundary.

Minis Azaka: Minis Azaka, or Minister Azaka, is the head of the farm — the owner and operator. Minis is the wealthy estate owner. He is often described in terms that would classify him as a Creole, or a mixed heritage individual. In the aftermath of the revolution, the tenable way of making income was to reinvest in the land, however it's very understandable why people who were enslaved to work on plantations would be hesitant and resistant to the idea of farming the same plantations for their own profit. These farms were called Komes, and were often run by the former *affranchi,* or enfranchised people of color. Komes, also known as *lakous*, support the traditional model of the structure of traditional religion. Minis represents the national economy, which to this day is a great example of a strong agricultural economy. Minis Azaka is the father and head of the Djuba nation of Lwa. He is married to the Lwa Azaka Amamu'ide, a water Lwa associated with the soft rains that water the fields and the flowering of fruits and vegetables, and with my favorite flower, the national flower of Haiti: the Hibiscus. Minis Azaka is a very shrewd and strict Lwa; he is very quick to address breaks from tradition. Minis Azaka is also an herbalist and knows *medicyn fay*, herbal medicine both spiritual and practical for wellness, and knows how to heal and hurt, and cross and cure with the sacred plants of the earth. This is a quality shared among many of the members of the Azaka family.

Azaka Mede: The son of Minis Azaka and Azaka Amamu'ide, he is the Lwa who is the patron of farmers. He is not necessarily a rich or wealthy landowner, but a fiscally frugal and successful farmer who is able to make do and feed his family from both the crops grown as well as what is sold in the marketplace. Azaka Mede is a diligent and extremely hard worker. He drives a hard bargain and must be treated with both honor and respect. He takes agreements very seriously. Azaka Mede demands honesty from his servitors while also not being totally honest with himself – he is known to steal and take things that do not belong to him in order to feed and support his family. During his celebrations, or in portions of the services, Azaka tend to come down in possession or incorporation in groups. They may argue amongst themselves, steal from one another, and hustle and sell to each other and to the attendants, but mostly they come to dance, instruct and bless, or to otherwise enjoy the time of their celebration. Aside from being the patron of farmers, he is also the patron of all working-class people, and 9-5 workers. Azaka Mede is the capacity for us to uncover the treasures of hard work during our walk on the great road. While his father, Minis Azaka, is wealthy, Azaka Mede stands to represent the peasant population. Unlike most of the male Lwa, Azaka Mede is not a *Met* or Master, he is a *Minis* or Minister. His position as minister makes him not the earth itself, but the management team of the earth. He has a sacred relationship to the land; he knows the secrets of the land and how to properly turn untamed land into usable, arable soil. Who he is minister to – that is the question. Orisha Oko is the fertile, full land of fruitful freshness where water is a blessing. Obaluaye is the dry earth, the spirit of disease and hot unwellness, where water is not always a blessing. These two forces can be clearly seen in the Lwa Azaka Krib and Kuzen Azaka Mede.

Kuzine Azaka Mede: The wife of Kuzen

Kuzine by Aarron Campbell

Azaka Mede, she is the merchant woman who goes to the marketplace to sell her husband's goods. She is the holder of money and provides loans and deals to people. She is a serious woman and should not be trifled with. She, unlike her husband and many of the male Azaka spirits, has a very loud and booming voice. She is one of my favorite Lwa in the Azaka family of Lwa. She is a mother and merchant; she in many ways is like Erzuli Dantor.

Kuzen Azaka Mede: the son of Azaka
Mede and the most familiar to many who know
of these Lwa. Kuzen, which means cousin, is
often used like the term 'Papa', which is a term
of respect and endearment. *Kuzen* is a term
used in Haiti to describe anyone with a level of
closeness, just like the term 'Uncle' and 'Aunt' in
Black American and other POC groups. Kuzen
is the peasant farmer who works and works to
make ends meet. He works from the crack of
dawn to the last light of the setting sun.

Kuzen Azaka by Aarron Campbell

Kuzen Azaka Mede

Azaka Tonner by C. Kline

Kuzen Azaka Mede is the Lwa of the average man in an agrarian economy. He is known by his straw hat and his work bag that is full of his tools, supplies, goods, and treasures. When in Incorporation, otherwise called Possession, he often has a nasally, squeaky voice, not unlike his brother Guede. Kuzen is one of the most popular Lwa in Haiti, as he understands and goes through the trials and tribulations of the average Haitian. He knows the back-breaking work of the field and furrow, he knows the hard work of making and preparing products to sell at the market, he knows how to keep his ear to the ground to make good deals that favor his bottom dollar and therefore his family.

He is a reflection of the peasant farmer, who can enjoy the simple things in life. This is understood, but not always believed. Kuzen is also a trickster Lwa, which is talked about less directly. Kuzen, like any wise man who lives in a restrictive market of scarcity, exists humbly and below his means but is indeed a key to unlocking the wealth of the earth. Kuzen, as he is known and as I have called him, is much like the term papa, only this time meaning 'cousin'. This is a term of respect and endearment. Everyone has a cousin who needs a loan, or one from whom you would perhaps not mind a loan yourself (if you don't think you have one of these cousins, you may in fact *be* that cousin).

Kuzen is a highly energetic Lwa who dances ecstatically and joyfully. At his parties and celebrations, he, much like Guede, often comes down in a number of people, unlike some other Lwa where the energy will coalesce in one of the ritual participants. This is not an exact science but is an often-observed situation. Kuzen is a Lwa who has a very large family, and many, many wives. It is very common to ritually marry Kuzen. *Maraj* or *Maraj Lwa* is the ritual act to have a tighter relationship with the Lwa.

There are many superstitions that come with this relationship, mostly due to the way that Haitian ideals cling to western ideology. It is important to remember that the Lwa are not 'Magic Ghosts' – that is to say, they are not physical humans, or even human. Kuzen is a field, a seed, the fruit, the tools, the stem, the market transaction, the noises, smells, tastes, actions and everything to do with the agrarian economy and farming lifestyle. The Lwa may act with, or take on the mannerisms of a human gender, but rest assured if you are a man, and Kuzen says you are supposed to marry him, it is not a romantic Victorian wedding. This is a business arrangement, not an exploration of homosexuality (unless you want it to be, but that's really not the exercise intended or implied). While this is uncommon, it happens; Damballa is a snake, he can also marry, but no one is anticipating or expecting you to take up a romantic relationship with a serpent, or any other non-human animal (unless that's your thing, but it's certainly not at Vodou's request).

Market by Alicia Anderson

Kuzen may be the center of the house and family, but his wife Kouzine Azaka Mede is the lifeblood of the family. What Kuzen makes and grows, Kouzine takes to the market and sells, this is because of the semblance of the egalitarian nature of Haiti and the semblance of freedom it has for women, despite the standing of the country as Catholic with all the pitfalls that presents to women everywhere. This was a way for women to gain and gather their own funds, because once the total amount expected was gained, the leftover proceeds made though good salesmanship were their own. Even in ceremony, when people have borrowed money from Kuzen or Minis Azaka, it is Kouzine who receives and handles the physical money. They both are hard workers and together reflect the heteronormative couple in Haiti.

To return to marriage again, romantic marriage is, and for the most part exists only in, a misty and lofty dream. Even today, many marriages in Haiti are ones of necessity that have to do more with mutual survival than with romance. This is not to say that romance does not occur, but some are not so fortunate. There are many pressures put on the average woman in Haiti, including to have children and to sate the needs and requests of men. The capacity to have sovereignty and power in relationships or the single life is found in Kouzine, and in many other Lwa such as Erzuli Dantor and Manze Marie. Together they are the spiritual mirror of the common person. They are the cousins, close or distant, that we all have.

Kuzen and Kouzine and the rest of the Djouba are greeted with the praise call 'Alaso'

'Alaso Lamiral' or 'Alaso Kuzen' in tandem with certain whistling patterns and vocalizations. Although the Djouba are served in the Rada section, they are not always saluted with the Asson, which is the tool associated with the royal priesthood of Dahomey and the deities from the Rada and Nago rites; instead, the Kwa Kwa or Tcha Tcha is used. This hints at two very large and intersecting points that may be clear already. Kuzen and Kouzine are not necessarily or overtly royal Lwa – they are unsophisticated Lwa who reflect the common people of Haiti.

The Tcha Tcha is a Taino religious tool, which not only points to part of their spiritual heritage but also to their relationship to the common people. The Asson is used for Lwa who have a relationship to kingship and regality, whereas the Tcha Tcha is used when addressing hotter Lwa who are closely related to Haiti and the revolution.

🐚

In Vodou all you need for almost anything are Water and Light, the primary necessities for life, after sustenance and shelter, which are two more principal concepts of Vodou. Light is frequently represented by use of a candle or *Balen*, but this is not used when saluting the Djouba Lwa, rather a *bouji* is used, which is anything but 'bougie'. A bouji is often twisted fabric soaked in a combination of colored paraffin wax and fat. When ignited it produces a high flame, similar to a Chinese style Hong zhu (red candle). These two, together with his herbaceous bottle of booze, his hat, and his bag are used to call to Kuzen to come down and stay for a bit of celebration.

Kuzen is very serious and does not like jokes or games. He treats people who break their word very strictly and can be very challenging to deal with if you owe him something. He takes theft very seriously and does not take losing anything well, even something that we would take for granted. Kuzen enjoys the fruits of his labors and must be the first to taste his food. Any food prepared, cooked, or set out for him must go untasted, as the taste by itself is considered theft. A scrap or a sliver of tobacco, the tiny taste of a morsel, the sip of alcohol not intended for you to taste, the small non-silver change of American coinage, all these things are noticed and accounted for. Kuzen is a strong Lwa and gives graciously to his children and devotees. He is known for making businesspeople very successful and for bringing windfalls into the lives of people who need it. Kuzen Azaka Mede is the Lwa who knows what it is like to live in hardship, with only the memory of good times. He has lived, and continues to live, a life of hard work and toil.

Terre Travay by Alicia Anderson

Saint Isidore and the Holy Trinity of Vodou

Isidro de Merlo y Quintana, or Saint Isidore, in contrast to the many other saint masks used to represent the Lwa, is actually a very fitting mask and hostage for this Lwa. Saint Isidore the Laborer was born in 1070 in Madrid, named in honor of the saint Isidore, Archbishop of Seville. He was born to a poor and humble family. Later in life he became a hired hand to a wealthy landowner called Juan de Vargas. He worked for Juan and was the steward of some of his land on the outskirts of Madrid. He married his wife, who is also a saint, Maria, and had one son, who also is a saint. There are five miracles attributed to him, recorded by a deacon named Juan in a work called *Códice de Juan Diácono*, *The Codex of John the Deacon*, or *Codice de San Isidoro*, *The Codex of Saint Isidore*. His love of animals and living things compelled him one winter to pour out some grain for some pigeons. He was admonished for this; however, when the sack of grain was taken to the mill it produced twice the amount of flour it should have.

Another miracle is attributed to his power of prayer. St. Isidore was going to a dinner that was being hosted for him by his *Confriada* or confraternity, which is often charitable and centered around a spiritual and religious doctrine. He arrived late and with a troop of needy and hungry people. His hosts were sure there was not enough food to feed St. Isidore, let alone his companions, but there was, in fact, enough food to feed everyone.

During the dog days of summer St. Isidore went to the church of St. Mary Magdalene. While he was inside praying, a group of villagers came into the church to warn Isidore that his donkey would soon become prey to a wolf; upon hearing this St. Isidore said, "My sons, go in peace, God's will be done." When he finally left the church, the wolf was found dead and the donkey unharmed.

The most famous of his miracles arose from the jealousy of his fellow workers. His coworkers complained to their lord Juan de Vargas. The next morning Isidore woke up before the sun and walked to each of the churches of Madrid and prayed at each one. Vargas believed the snitches and scolded Isidore and proceeded to watch him work. Isidore prayed to God, hitched up his oxen, and set to plough. All of a sudden from the heavens two white oxen appeared, and behind the plough, an angel. Vargas saw this, and saw the angel, and the team of two white oxen vanished as Isidore's work was completed. Seeing this, Vargas apologized to Isidore, and Isidore knew this miracle had happened though God.

While I in no way think the saint is the Lwa or the Lwa the saint, each of the miracles does reflect some of the nature of the Azaka family of spirits and especially that of Kuzen himself, namely his ability to feed the needy, his ability to make a lot from a little, his ability to protect or have protection over livestock, and not to mention his divine help to lighten the load of his labor. Kuzen is the constant laborer – his work is never finished, just simply done for now.

Kuzen is an incredibly hard worker and is both the bounty of the earth and its ability to provide, as well as the natural miracle of the abundance of the total Earth. The Djouba spirits are the ones who drew our ancestors away from the full-time seasonal job of hunting, to growing the fruits of the field and forests and to the slower lives of growing crops and cereals which developed our brains and built communities and their traditions.

The holy trinity of Vodou is the heteronormative family: Father, Mother, and Child, usually a son. This is reflective of the Catholic tradition while also respecting the way that the ancestors and family powers are balanced and maintained. Saint Isidore, his wife, and son are all saints.

Right Relationship with the Land, and the Mystery of the Soil

Kuzen, like many of the Lwa, is one who helps when one takes responsibility by the horns. A hard-working spirit cares little for the lazy, or those slow to action. Kuzen, as previously mentioned, is the Lwa that represents our ability to find and make use of the treasures and things we find on Earth. He represents what we can make for ourselves through our hard work, through our struggle, through our desire to elevate the conditions and situations of our life. Kuzen can be a little paradoxical, which should not be shocking to those paying attention. Kuzen Azaka Mede is both poor and rich. How can you be both? Kuzen is the ultimate provider, while also living in extreme lack – how can this be so? It depends on what side of the story you are on. Those he is close to or claims, either by their head in initiation, their hand in *Maraj* or marriage, or who are otherwise present in the court of this Lwa, are those he treasures and with whom he shares his gifts willingly. If you are not in these lists, how do you get there? The answer is through hard work and the strength to show you care about your standing with the earth, the land you are on, and the people around you.

Right Relationship is a concept that was taught to me by Lora O'Brien of the Irish Pagan School. Right Relationship is when your actions, way and being are in accordance and proper balance with the world around you, and the beings who also share that space. This concept is often talked about with the idea of Sovereignty. This idea is not a stranger to Vodou, or to many of the African Diasporic Traditions whose main and primary initiations are coronation ceremonies. To have the right relationship with the land means that the treasures and bounties of the land can be or are unblocked. In many tales from Ireland's folklore, we see examples of this, especially in the *Lebor Gabála Érenn*, or the *Book of the Taking of Ireland*, commonly known as the *Book of Invasions*. When individuals who claim Ireland do so with the right relationship, rivers and fields spring up, while those who do not have the right relationship do not experience this effect of the land assisting them. Kuzen Azaka Mede, to me, is the judge of this ability when it comes to the subject of right relationship with the land and earth in Haiti.

Like all mountainous places, one side of the mountain will be drier than the other. Haiti is that side, the 'desert' side of the mountains. The ability to work the land of Haiti, and to live off it, is a task – not as monumental as some may think, but still a trial. Right Relationship was not had by the Europeans, and the first hurricane season they weathered there on Hispaniola destroyed all the crops and food-bearing plants.

Kuzen is the Lwa of work, skill, and trade; Kuzen is the spirit who stands in to represent the force of back-breaking, hard, challenging work. Kuzen is the one who manages and maintains the land for us, he is the minister to the bounty of the ancient earth. He is the one who whispers to the small plants to grow or recede into the soil, he is the one who whispers to the birds to stay or fly away. Kuzen is watching our interactions with each other and knows the flow of power. Kuzen rewards the honest and plain. The Djouba nation are known for their work ethic, ability to provide, and above all to manage the financial affairs of the world — they are also renowned for another skill: their dancing and drumming. May first is the Haitian holiday of *Fête du Travail,* or Labor

Day or Celebration of Labor. This is the day for farmers to take a break after the harvest is in. It is common in farming communities to come together to ensure a full harvest for everyone. This kind of work in Haiti has a name, *Konbit*, which can have several meanings: used as a verb, it means 'to put your hands together'; as a noun, it means 'communal or cooperative labor'. *Konbit* is the community coming together, which is how it is possible for people to perform colossal feats like bringing in hectares of cane, corn, or other crops. When this work is done the community comes together to celebrate the efforts of the collective.

I am sure many people have experienced this kind of celebration, which sometimes replaces payment. We have all packed, or moved, or unpacked, or all three for a friend, family member, or friend of a friend with a pick-up truck, for a pizza, beer, or other form of takeaway. In Haiti this may also include a drum and dance session. The drumming style of the Djouba is fierce and energetic and can be played in several different ways. The *Maman* drum, the drum that leads the rest of the drums, can be played standing or lying upon its side; it can also be played with the introduction of a foot on top of the hand and mallet used to play the drum. The dance itself is a quick-footed style dance. This dance step made it all over the New World. Another area to which the Djouba people were taken was my second favorite city in the South, Charleston, South Carolina. Here the Djouba's dance grew famous and has been known as 'Juba' or 'Pattin' Juba'. These motions and steps were used in minstrel shows and would eventually influence other areas of dance like Tap and Jazz. The Juba dance was brought into the spotlight by the African American master dancer, William Henry Lane, known as 'Master Juba', who performed with minstrel performers across the USA and Europe. The dance of the Haitian Djouba is fast paced with fancy footwork, and is, as I like to call it, Haitian Square Dance.

Kuzen Azaka Mede and the Orisha

The Rada *'Nancion'*, or nation, is one large group composed of smaller groups, including the Nago nation, where the Ogou spirits are found, as well as the Adja, Mina, and Djouba spirits. These members of the extended Rada family exhibit strong traits associated with their culturally relative morals. We see this in the importance the family structure holds for the Azaka family of spirits, and we see that the traditional order of the Haitian household is also central: the masculine role is the turning of the soil and preparing the land for planting and harvesting, which may or may not include female participation. The role of Kuzen Azaka Mede's wife, Kuzine Azaka Mede, is to manage the home and household.

Kuzen is known for his fecundity and is known to be a bit of a lady's man, with many wives and many children. In some lineages of Vodou there is a mysterious figure that sits at the head of the Azaka Djouba family of spirits.

Orisha Oko, or Olicha Oko, is a divinity closely associated with the Yoruba people. Orisha Oko is worshiped by the Aborishas and Olorishas of the tradition of Lucumi, who venerate him as an agricultural divinity whose fertility is shown by his large testicles. Kuzen and Orisha Oko share a similar food offering. Orisha Oko's offering is called *ajïaco*, Kuzen's is called *tchaka*; this is a hearty stew made with many root vegetables, and can have meat, fish, and other ingredients added to it. Orisha Oko, and another Orisha, Sakpata, share a relationship with Kuzen Azaka Mede, and in particular with the Lwa Minis Azaka Mede.

Kuzen is in many ways is the representation of the average peasant farmer in Haiti. He is their champion because of his ability to be fruitful and live off the land. A part of that success is the ability to recognize, assess, and destroy the obstacles that stand before him. Farming is a job that has a lot of risk: the chance of drought can destroy crops, too much rain can flood crops, and not enough land for grazing means larger animals raised for meat won't be able to survive. Another issue that has faced farmers for both help and hurt is the chance that foul witchcraft and sorcery have been used to affect their livelihood and ability to thrive. The detection of witchcraft and magic is one of the great skills that Kuzen has. Kuzen is a straightforward, no-bullshit guy who doesn't want to deal with foolish time-consuming things like a jealous neighbor. Kuzen is not just a farmer, but also a spiritual adept. Kuzen is the SCUD missile to use against any kind of magic or spell-craft that has been buried or otherwise interred in the earth. Likewise, just as much as this power can be used for good, it can also be used to harm or defend. Kuzen, as the minister of the earth, has a relationship with the forces that were believed to emanate from the ground. Many people believed that disease rose from the earth like a miasmic gas, or 'bad air', thus the term 'malaria' comes from the Italian *mala aria*, or literally *bad air*. The earth holds the ability to reward or to ruin you, based on the kinds of interactions you have and your relationship to the forces of the earth.

Kuzen Azaka Mede is very close and very similar to Guede. Guede parties hard because he had to work all his life, while his brother works and celebrates the harvest once a year. We only get the reward if we stay alert and work. In Vodou, as in many things (dare I say all things), you reap what you sow. Sure, some get it easy, but for others it is difficult. Kuzen is the journey of finding and using the treasures we uncover and grow during our lifetime on earth. Kuzen also represents not only our need to feed ourselves but also *how* we feed ourselves: the grain maize was brought to the African continent several years before the slave trade began, so many would have been familiar with this food from home; okra was carried in seed form in the hair of our great-great-grandmothers to plant and sustain us in the new world; yam, the distant cousin of the potato, was so ubiquitous a food to our ancestors that its name *is* food; the rice plant, from the short grain to the Carolina long grain enjoyed the world over and for whose sake many people were brought to the New World across the sea of the dead to raise and grow from humble beginnings, was cultivated for its starchy goodness; sugar squash, beans, melon, fruits of the earth, the humble plantain, coconut, chayote, and the feathers and fur, hoof, and trotter raised by our care.

Colors, Fabrics, and Devotional Spaces

Minis Azaka: Green, Blue
Kuzen Azaka Mede: Red, Blue, Denim
Azaka Krib: Red, Green, Burlap
Kuzine: Denim, Gingham (any color), Blue

Red: Blood, sacrifice, sustenance, the enrichment of blood into soil.
Blue: Water, life giving energy, hottest flame.
Green: The fullness of life, the green of chlorophyll, the subtle in the gross.
Cool blackness: the unknown.

Setting up a sacred space for Kuzen in your home

Kuzen is a humble spirit and does not need or want the fanciest things around. It is important for a Lwa like Kuzen to earn through working his materials; the whole point of venerating Kuzen is that the both of you should be going up at the same time, so that when you increase, he increases. I also suggest starting off slow with him; feel him out, start off small and work your way to bigger items. It is easy to get carried away; just remember to keep cool and keep focused.

You will need:

A small table, or a section of an already existing Rada shrine or Vodou altar.

Fay/Plants
Baton/Staff
Chapo/Hat
Makout/bag
Lajan/Money
Kwi/Gourd bowl
Gode/Tin cup
Bouty/bottle
Mushwa/Scarf
Zouti/Tools
Tiwo et Tobac/
Tobacco and corn
cob pipe

Kuzen Azaka Mede

Food Offerings, Recipes, and Baths

Many of what are thought of as quintessential or heraldic items of Vodou are products that are from the New World, and many were shown to us by Native Americans. Tobacco and rum, just to name two, are inseparable from the idea of Vodou.

Tchaka:

2 cups of dried corn
3 corn on the cob, broken
½ calabaza, or Caribbean pumpkin
2 chayote/mirliton
1 yucca
2 cups of red beans
2 cups of kidney beans
1 lb of beef/pork
2 salt cured pig feet, sliced, or a ham hock
Fresh thyme
Fresh parsley
White pepper

7 garlic cloves
1 medium onion
1 bell pepper
5 bay leaves
Juice of 2 sour oranges
Juice of 1 lime
Pepper to taste

The night before, set the beans to soak. Peel and chop all the vegetables; with a little oil, brown the beef or pork; with the onions and garlic add the rest of the meat and vegetables, seasoning, stock, and water. Let it simmer most of the day, serve with rice.

Lalo, Fey Legume:

2 lbs of beef, diced in chunks.
1 lime
2 tsp of black pepper
1 tsp of garlic powder
A few sprigs of fresh rosemary
A few sprigs of thyme
3-4 sprigs of parsley
3 cubes of Maggi chicken bouillon
1 cup of oil
2 tsp of epis, or sofrito

Kuzen Azaka Mede

1 can of tomato paste
Garlic, pepper, rosemary, thyme, Maggi or
bouillon cubes
1 bell pepper
1 onion
1 box of frozen chopped spinach
6 bags of frozen jute leaves
Water as needed
White rice

Clean the meat with the juice of half a lime.
Season with black pepper, garlic powder,
rosemary, thyme, parsley, chicken bouillon cubes,
and epis. Squeeze the other half of the lime juice
over the meat. Drizzle with oil. Let it marinate.

Transfer the meat into a saucepan over high
heat. Add 2 quarts of water. Continue to cook
over medium-high heat until tender and the
water has evaporated. Set aside the meat. In the
same saucepan, add one can of tomato paste. Stir
in onions and bell peppers. Sauté over high heat.
Reduce heat to medium-high. Add in 6 cups
of water, the jute leaves (*lalo*), and the chopped
spinach. Stir in rosemary, thyme, parsley. Let it
cook for 20-30 minutes. Taste and adjust to add
more seasonings as needed. Combine the cooked
meat into the vegetables.

If you are cooking for Kuzen Azaka Mede, Minis Azaka, or any of the Djuba Lwa, do **not** taste the food before giving them their portion.

Baths

Prosperity bath:

Basil
Rice water
Orange peel, or leaves and peel
Banana
Apple
Spinach
Cinnamon and Star Anise

Orient all the items of the bath and pray earnestly to Kuzen and the Lwa about what you need and what you are trying to accomplish. In a pot, place about a cup of white rice in water and agitate the water until it takes on a white color. Strain the rice from the water, add cinnamon and star anise and set to boil; when boiled, set to cool.

Fill another basin halfway with cool water. Cut up the apple and the banana, tear up the spinach and basil in the water until it turns green.

Add the spiced rice water. Burn a candle by the bath and bathe after the candle goes out. Take the bath after a regular cleaning shower, allowing yourself to air dry as much as possible.

Luck bath (good for job finding):

Basil
Banana leaves
Florida Water
Reve D'or perfume
Red Door perfume
Bright colored flower petals
Corn meal
21 coins
21 dollars
Fresh milk
Honey

Orient all the items of the bath and pray earnestly to Kuzen and the Lwa about what you need and what you are trying to accomplish. In a clean basin of water crush the basil and banana leaves, and add the perfume, cornmeal, milk, honey, the colored flowers, and the money, choosing the coins first followed by the notes or bills. Burn a candle by the bath and bathe after the candle goes out. Take the bath after a regular cleaning shower, allowing yourself to air dry as much as possible.

Uncrossing/Curse Breaking bath:

Fay asosi/Bitter-melon herb
Quita maldicion/Grey knickerbean
Basil
Mint
Fay loupgarou/Mother of thousands
Purslane
Coconut water
Salt

Orient all the items of the bath and pray earnestly to Kuzen and the Lwa about what you need and what you are trying to accomplish. To a clean basin of water add the coconut water. Crush all the herbs into the bath. Liberally add salt. Light four white candles in a cross with the bath at the center. Take the bath after a regular cleaning shower, allowing yourself to air dry as much as possible. Have the remains of the bath taken to a trash can outside your home.

Prayers and Songs

Prayer:

Azaka Mede o evi Dahomey!
Azaka Mede o evi Dahomey!
Evi Dahomey, evi gweto!
Evi Dahomey, evi gweto!
Azaka Mede, hounfo evi djo e!

Minis Azaka:

Minis Azaka n'ape di'w bonswa!
O bonswaaa-o Minis-o!
Kouzen Zaka n'ape di'w bonswa!
O bonswa-o Minis-o!
Azaka Mede n'ape di'w bonswa ... Azaka
Gweliye n'ape di'w bonswa ... Zaka Kwesi n'ape
di'w bonswa ... Kouzen e Kouzin n'ape di'w
bonswa! O bonswaaa-o Minis-o!
Zaka ki kote'w prale?
Minis Zaka ki kote'w prale la? Azaka Mede
m'pral nan pakoti-e move tan'n bare mwen!

Kuzen Azaka Mede:

Travay m'ap travay O
Kouzin Zaka, m'ap travay ou tande! (x2)
Kouto digo-m nan men-m Djakout mwen
sou do-m/M'ap sekle/Kouto digo-m nan men-m
Vye alfo-m sou do-m
M-ap sekle
Jou m gen youn fanm, l'ale kite m
Demen m'a jwen yon lot o!
Travay, ma'p Travay m'ap travay ave!Zaka
mete travay! (x2)
M' pat pansesi' m te ka fe travay sa yo
Zaka mete' m travay la nan bitasyon mwen

Kuzen Azaka Mede:

Azaka si Azaka la, Azaka Mede!
Azaka si Azaka la, Azaka Mede!
Azaka bobo ile,Azaka bobo ile,
Azaka Kreyol manje rezon mwen.

Kuzen Azaka Mede:

Kouzen-ooo nèg mwen!
Azaka Mede-o nèg mwen! (bis)

Gad'oun ane w'ap resi manje tande! Nan peyi isit w'ap resi manje tande!

Azaka Mede wi nèg mwen

Kouzen Azaka Mede:

Bonswa kouzen bonswa kouzin o
Ayaya kouzen (x2)
Jan yo wè-m nan konsa danjere

Tout Djouba:

Onè respe, Onè respe (x2)
Si mwen te konen patadi onè sila
Ma leve moun sa yo sou do mwen

Workings

To call Kuzen Azaka Mede, and how to prepare a plot of land or growing space for him and other members of the Djouba nation

You will need:

Tobacco and a corncob pipe
Dried corn, beans, rice
Yucca
Whiskey
Kiman
Viable living seeds of vegetables, (or herbs, culinary over medicinal),
A small place to plant and grow the seeds, can be a window box or a planter, or a simple plant pot, or even something larger; Kuzen works with and for the land.
Denim, bandanas, burlap, or other similar fabric.
A shovel

4 small candles

Kwa kwa/tcha tcha (washed or unwashed)

Present all the collected items above, find a
suitable spot of earth, and consider what plants
are growing there. Is it a natural spot, or carefully
manicured? Is the plant life growing around it
similar or different? While having a candle lit,
salute Kuzen. Pour three drops of whiskey for
Kuzen with the kiman added within the bottle
of whiskey. This bottle should be kept separate
from the rest of your liquor collection. Kiman
is an often-herbal concoction that is the spiritual
essence of the Lwa, but in plant, mineral, and
biological form. The whiskey that the kiman is
put in is transmuted from the mundane to the
spiritual. No longer is the whiskey just a suitable
beverage; it becomes the energetic liquid body
of the Lwa in a distant but relative way. The
process is made whole when words and actions
are performed. Be sure to present the bottle
to area the before you, behind you, to the east
and west, with the bottle in one hand, and a
candle or *bouji* in the other. Cover this bottle
with bandanas, denim, burlap, gingham. When
speaking to Kuzen, support yourself – speak to
him with confidence and clarity, and speak out

loud to him that you're seeking his presence in your journey. Tell him in what way you want to see this happen.

From the area that you have poured the libation, take a shovel and dig up a goodly amount of the soil there. You don't need a lot, just enough to mix into other soil and planting products. If you are doing this on your own land, or land that is suitable, or where it is ok to dig deep, dig a hole two feet deep or so. Spread the soil that is taken from the hole evenly around the opening, put four of the candles around the hole like the points of a compass: one north, another each south, east and west, and be sure to separate any stones, root chunks, rubble or other non-soft dirt materials, setting them aside for now. With another section of fabric take the tobacco, the pipe, the dried corn, beans, rice, and the yucca and tie them in a bundle, orient them, salute with them, and place them in the hole. Pour another three-drop libation and salute the hole. Fill in the hole and place the stones and roots and other obstructions on top of the hole. One could maintain this spot as an outdoor shrine for this Lwa. Otherwise, with the soil you have taken with you, create with that soil and supplementary soil a planter, window box, or other similar situation;

plant the seeds, keep life growing and going. Any fully matured vegetables should, or can, be used to feed yourself and others, or to make offerings.

To attract business or buyers:

You will need:

Wampum corn/Decorative, colorful autumn corn

A candle, whiskey, and water

4 largest denomination coins, 4 small, and 4-8 bills of whatever value you choose.

Green, blue, and red ribbons or hemp string

Saint Isidore the Laborer chromolithograph or a printed picture or drawing.

Dried wormwood

Green, blue, or red fabric

With all the materials, orient and salute Kuzen, the Lwa, Legba, and the ancestors, pouring the libations of water and whiskey. If you know any songs for Legba, sing them, and transition naturally into songs for Kuzen. Take the three ribbons and three strands of hemp string and braid them together. Make a small bag from the fabrics and in each bag place a coin of lesser and of greater denomination, wrapped in a bill or note, while also including wormwood, and secure them to the braided ribbon or hemp strings. Tie them to the corn, spray with the whiskey and set it aside. On the back of the chromolithograph write, in the form of a letter to Kuzen, that you need to work and earn money in some way and ask him to see you through, making an offer to him on what you will do when you have achieved a level of sustainable success. Frame the chromolithograph, set the corn bundle and the letter next to a candle and water for the evening until dawn next day. Hang this in your business or in the area your business takes place.

Lamps

To strike a deal with Minis Azaka:

You will need:
Twa pied, *cho dye*, 3-legged cauldron, or fire pot
Olive oil
Castor oil
Palm oil
Honey

Salt
A cotton wick
Silver, gold, or high denomination of coin
Dried corn
Bull/cow/bovine horn shavings

To make an offering:
White yam
Frying oil

With all the materials gathered, orient and salute Minis Azaka (follow my directions in *Papa Legba: A Workbook* on how to make lamps), float the cotton wick over or on top of the coin. Under the coin, put a dab of honey and salt. Add the corn, no more than seven kernels. Just a pinch of the horn powder is required. Add the three oils. Dig a small hole, or place safely on the ground. You can float this lamp in a basin of water, but to burn it on dry ground is best. Below the lamp place your petition – you should make sure to read it out loud after the lamp is lit. Sing songs and pray out loud even if all you know are Hail Mary's and Our Fathers. Tell Minis Azaka what you need and what you will do when you get it. Be sure to follow through when it happens – it doesn't matter how it happens, once it happens

Kuzen Azaka Mede

don't forget. As an initial offering to support your request peel a white yam and boil it until soft, add a little flour and mash the yam, and roll it into balls. Heat foil to frying temperature and fry the balls until golden brown.

To break witchcraft:

You will need:
A broken mirror shard
Small stones from a garden
Quita maldicion
A crab shell
A coconut shell
A cotton wick
Palm oil
Almond oil

On a brown piece of paper write your name, or in the case of breaking spiritual work which has been done on a piece of land, write the name of the estate. If no name is known, write the address and the name of the primary owner of the land; if there is more than one owner and they are married write both names side by side in order of who purchased the land, first name followed by surname.

An example name paper if the afflicted is one individual:

Sam Rodgers

An example name paper if the afflicted is land, and the owner is single:

123 Willoughby Road, West Youngstown 47141
Nowhereland USA Sam Rodgers

An example name paper if the afflicted is land and the owner is married, and was so during the acquisition of the land:

123 Willoughby Road, West Youngstown 47141
Nowhereland USA Sam Martha Rodgers

If Martha had bought the land before Sam, her name would appear first.

Write the following around the names above, below, to the left and the right:

*ALASO*K.T.K.M.K.D.P.*ALASO*

Kuzen Azaka Mede

Fill the rest of the name paper with specific sacred symbols pertaining to the situation at hand, and the individual or location.

You can use good powders, herbs, oils, waters, and what have you; if you know what to use, then do so when making the name paper and envelope. Otherwise, in the bottom of the coconut shell place all the materials except the oils, with the broken mirror shard on the top. Float the wick in the oils and set to light in the earth. I encourage you to let the whole lamp burn, so this lamp is best done outdoors, and in a place where it is fine to dig a hole, and fine to have more or less an open flame. Please do not leave fires unattended, and please remember to bring something to extinguish the fire if it gets out of hand. If the fire gets out of hand, chances are you need some professional assistance and should not be trying to do this on your own.

Anacaona, The Butterfly in the Forest, The Golden Flower: Lwa of Passion and Wisdom

Anacaona, as previously mentioned, was the last Taino queen of Quisqueya. She is venerated throughout the Antilles. Anacaona is honored in Regleman between La Siren and Erzuli Freda; she is a Lwa of passion and love, probably moreso than Erzuli Freda, who is really a Lwa of chance and destiny. Anacaona in possession is wild and graceful. She will unceremoniously pounce upon and overpower men in the room when in possession. She is a joyful being who dances with power and grace. She is a coquettish wonder woman – she loves fiercely and protects women and children. If you are familiar with Lwa like La Rein Kongo and the 21 Divisions Lwa Anaisa Pye, she acts very similar to her when in possession. Her center of worship is in the city of Leogan, which is also a center of worship of Erzuli Freda. In the center of the city is a statue of Anacaona surrounded by the zemi. Anacaona is an expert healer and diplomatic peacekeeper. In life she was a religious expert, she was a poet, and had wisdom and knowledge on her side. She is a Lwa of love, freedom, wisdom, and power, not to mention a priestess and magician who can pass on magical and spiritual wisdom to people who listen and respect knowledge and learning. In many ways she is like a Guede: she loves life and living and the *ability* to live as much as she loves life itself. An animal associated with her is the butterfly, which flies freely and can be hard to follow. Anacaona is also known for frustrating the colonizers' plans and attempts to catch her. She would be spotted on one mountain, only to be found on another mountain, as if she had the ability to grow wings and fly away.

Anacaona is the Lwa who is the key to the mysteries of the island itself. She knew in life the spirits of the yucca cassabe plant, Yúkiyu Bagua Maórokoti, who we have to thank for the entire Amazon river basin. If you ever have bragged about your ayahuasca journeys, or any other traditional spiritual medicine, you owe it to this plant; without yucca, cassabe, or manioc there would be none of this. She knew Atabey, the zemi of the earth, fresh water, and fertility, without whom nothing would exist here. She

Kuzen Azaka Mede

knew the zemi Juracán, from which the word 'Hurricane' derives; this zemi, who is the child of Guabanex, the wild mother of rushing wind and water, would fight with Yúkiyu at the peaks of the forest in El Yunque, in Boriken, in what is today known as Puerto Rico. She knew Ceiba, the zemi of the Sacred Trees of Life, which were the portals and way places to the ancestors. She venerated these and many more zemi, including the *Opia*, the ancestors, and the *Maboya*, spirits that hunt at night to destroy crops and steal children and women, and who can be known by their lack of a belly button as they have never been born. She knew all the spirits, plants, and animals that live in the ecosystem of the greater and lesser Antilles.

It is she and her people that we, the inheritors of Vodou in Haiti, as well as many of the African Diasporic traditional religions, have to thank for many of the basic things we take for granted, like knowledge of local herbs, the planting of ceiba trees, the use of stones as idols, and devotional shrine objects in almost all of the folk traditions, Diasporic traditions, and much more. Vodou naturally is Afro-centric, but we cannot forget that they are not the only ones who were made servant and subject to the

Europeans. Although their stories are different, there is a lot of similarity between the struggle of the native people of Haiti and the continued struggle today of the Haitian Revolution. The Africans are the inheritors and stewards of the entire North American continent, and in particular the Haitians and all enslaved people on the island: their descendants were and are the inheritors and stewards of that land. It is through the blood, sweat, and tears of the black women, men and children, and native women, men and children, that the whole island eats, breathes, builds, and grows today.

The Taino are not dead, the zemi are not dead. The Taino assimilated and are interwoven into the fabric of all the cultures that were built in the Greater and Lesser Antillies. They are assimilated and interwoven into the Lwa, Orisha, Fodouse, Mpungo, Nkisi, Mysterio and all the Saints and folkloric beings of the Greater and Lesser Antillies. Anacaona is a window into a lost world from which we can only hope to take in but a glimmer of the secrets, mysteries, and knowledge she holds and will share. It all begins with water and light.

A small service to Anacaona:

You will need:

An unglazed clay vessel

A table, with yellow, white, or brown table coverings and other appropriate decorations.

A stone from a river or other freshwater source

Yellow and orange flowers: sunflowers, tiger lilies, marigolds,

Yellow, white and brown candles

Seafood, or a fish

Fresh water

Yucca or cassava prepared as food.

Honey

Fine tobacco or cannabis

Sweet perfume

'Unclaimed' *Kwa Kwa* or *Tcha Tcha*

Outside, or in an area that receives a lot of sunlight, set up a small table. This does not have to be a permanent installation; however, if you are going to make a permanent installation, I would follow the same regulations. Be sure to give some attention to Legba so he opens the doors for you. Decorate the table with the appropriate items and symbols which can be found by following these instructions. Keep the center clear for the clay jar. If you are lucky enough to live around a river (any will do, size or strength does not matter, just that water flows) collect from it a stone. This does not have to be a huge stone, it just has to be the right stone – you will know it when you find it. If you do not live near a river, do not rush. You will eventually come across one when the time is right. Place the stone in the earthenware jug, and in chalk, cascarilla, clay, or paint, draw the symbol below on the container. Fill it with water, orient or present this to the four corners: north, south, east, and west. Place some of the flowers in the container, talk to the Lwa, and greet her like you are greeting one who is rising from sleep. Slowly shake the Kwa Kwa while talking to her; if you are using feathers or a feather fan, begin to stir the air around the container, blow smoke, sprinkle sweet perfumes, and drizzle an amount of honey in the container and on the flowers. Ask this Lwa to come to you in dreams and to accept the offering and the humble beginnings of a relationship. Keep the table set up for at least twenty-four to forty-eight hours, take away any food offerings that have an offensive smell or are attracting bugs. Keep only the stone and vessel, and any honey, perfume and smoking comestibles. In time if you build a relationship with this Lwa, an appropriate image can be gotten for them. Be sure to keep the offering fresh, and to refresh the water in the container.

Colors:
Brown, Yellow, Orange

Offerings and Libations:
Shrimp, Crab, Snail, Fish, Turtle, Quail, Turkey, Champagne, Klaren, Honey, Cinnamon, Cloves, Star Anise

Sacred symbols:
Butterfly, Parrot, Hispaniola Trojan Hummingbird, Hibiscus, Royal Palm, healing leaves

Final Words

In the West a lot of things are taken for granted. Some of the most overlooked but necessary and essential products, fresh fruit and vegetables, are harvested by migrant workers. These people come to the United States, Canada, and other nations to perform back-breaking work in the fields in return for payment that is severely under the basic minimum wage. Often these workers are abused or face unacceptably harsh circumstances, and out of all that is harvested, only the few fruits and vegetables that are cosmetically pleasing to the consumer eye are chosen for distribution. Not only is this a waste of human effort, but it is also a waste of decent food. No one should go without while there is ample to go around, but how does this tie into Kuzen and the Azaka family?

It is easy to forget the cost of human life, it is easy to forget that for many of us who live in North, South, and Central America that we live on stolen land, and to this day the oppression of the original people of this land continues to happen. Recently the bodies of Native American children sent to residential schools for 're-education' to lose their unique culture have been found – more than 5,000 individuals. To this very day native First Nations women in Canada go missing without a trace. To this very day native men go missing only to reappear sterilized or mutilated so they are unable to reproduce. The fact that this goes on in our modern era is outrageous, but sadly not unthinkable. While we citizens have hopefully concluded that these treatments are wrong, some members of the governments we assist in forming through voting or not voting do not share this mindset. I know within my lifetime the veil of good PR will drop and the cruelty and inexcusable behavior of the Canadian government will be exposed, and that through embarrassment alone the five hundred year-old war against the Native Americans will end. I talk about right relationship to the land in this book. Having right relationship with the land requires more than not littering and respecting the plant and animal life; it also requires respecting the humans who inhabit, or once inhabited the land. The land is not our slave. We are subject to its unique needs and ways of expression; we should

Kuzen Azaka Mede

learn to work with the land to discover its unique regional voice. This is what Kuzen can teach us. The next time you eat a strawberry in December or a pea in November, remember the sacrifice that went into the harvest of that food.

Appendix 1: Taino Words[4]

Areito: Taino ceremony that includes song, music, dance, and history
barbacoa: a 4-legged stand made of sticks used for cooking; barbecue
batea: large tray
batey: yard area
bohio: typical round home of Tainos
Borikén: Great Land of the Valiant and Noble Lord
burén: flat cooking plate or griddle
cabuya: fishing line
cacique: chief
canarís: water vessels
caney: square house for Chiefs and Shamans only
canoas/piraguas/cayucas/kurialas: canoes
Caribe: strong people
casabi: yuca bread

---

4 This list is mostly from *Taino Words in the Puerto Rican Vocabulary*, website, El Boricua.com, 2021, <http://www.elboricua.com/vocabulary.html>.

cibucanes: used to extract poisonous juice from Yuca

coa: farming tool, a wooden stick used to work the soil

cokí/coqui: small tree frog

colibrí: hummingbird

conuco: farming area, mounds of loose soil

cucubano: lightning bug

ditas y jitacas: food vessels made from *higüero*

dujo: chair with short legs

fotuto: sea shell trumpet

guanín: chief's medallion

Guaraguao: red tailed hawk

guatiao: exchanging names and becoming blood brothers

iguana: lizard

Inrirí: woodpecker

jamaca: hammock

jicotea: land turtle

jurakan: storm

jutía: small rabbit-like creature

Lukiyó: sacred mountain

mabí: fermented drink made from the Mabí tree

macana: weapon, club

mime: small fly

nagua: loin cloth used by married women

nasa: fishing mesh or net

natiao: brothers
tabacú: tobacco
uguaca: parrot
yucayeque: Taino village
zabana: sheet

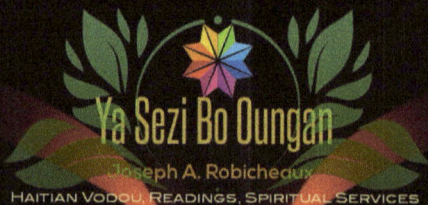

www.ingramcontent.com/pod-product-compliance
Lightning Source LLC
Chambersburg PA
CBHW071338290326
41933CB00039B/1666